WATER·SPRITE:

Songs for the God of Small Things

Water Sprite

Poems by
Luo Ying

Translated by Denis Mair

WHITE PINE PRESS / BUFFALO, NEW YORK

White Pine Press
P.O. Box 236
Buffalo, NY 14201
www.whitepine.org

Publication of this book was supported by public funds from the New York State Council on the Arts, with the support of Governor Kathy Hochul and the New York State Legislature, a State Agency.

Book design: Elaine LaMattina

Printed and bound in the United States of America.

ISBN 978-1-945680-74-8

Library of Congress Control Number: 2024930188

Contents

WATER·SPRITE:
Songs for the God of Small Things

MULTICOLORED FISH

My view into the distance flows like water
A multicolored fish leaps and lurks within time
Zither notes sound like limp, mottled leaves
A horse lingers where it strayed from its herd
In that far place I will not halt my steps
I walk on a whim to any corner of the world
Where everything slowly congeals, I quiet down
And listen to flowing sounds in the distance
This moment . . . a little squirrel falls asleep
As for me . . . in obscurity I light a single candle

December 24, 2010

PASSING TIME

I like the way passing time turns to pebbles
At times catching gleams of light, at times without shape
Walk on a mountain path, you'll hear it singing
Enter a jungle, it will sound like birds' calls
These are part of me and part of time
A thousand years since, a thousand years hence
I walk gingerly to keep from crushing leaves and things
Walking through time, my heart is always full of tenderness
Having gathered a strand of my wife's long hair
I whistle a tune into the depths of a dewdrop
The sound passes through thickets then hides within time
A doe has been lured into a clearing by the sound
Mystery is in her eyes; her breath has a honeyed scent

December 24, 2010

89TH PARALLEL OF THE COSMOS

Here I am at the 89th parallel of the cosmos, a trekker
Having walked past a tiny corner of the world
Like an old man who doesn't care if his chest cold improves
Or a deer trainer employed by God. I've learned
To comb and braid a young girl's hair
One afternoon I open the gate to the path
Let her do whatever she pleases
Having been at the 89th parallel of the cosmos
I will not rejoin the world's illusions
I will no longer tread on my own footprints
At the sight of a huge tree I look upward
High above . . . at barely visible slivers of light

December 24, 2010

TEARS OF A SPIDER

At twilight the dangling of spiders is of no consequence
They seem to bring odd messages from afar
Anchored by threads to parched leaves in a golden canopy
They appear as symbols of the beauty in this world
Autumn winds stir and vibrate their webs of silk
Spiders face the sun with their clawing limbs
They're poised like tears of the sun but don't roll down
To wait in such suspense would make hair turn white
I imagine myself a brother to the spider
Catching sunset's rays, I wish to gleam brightly
To capture all the glints and glances around me
Then quiet down . . . take my time . . . savor

December 24, 2010

GRASS

Grass, having yellowed could break off anytime
     Which is fine
for nest-building birds to get through winter
Staying warm through cold spells in little nooks
     Which is fine
It shows that this world is not too frigid
Under three feet of frozen ground,
a marmot dreams through his days
     Which is fine
He has a cache of seeds down there to sleep on
An oxcart lumbers, the road stretches like a thread
In stillness I observe the terrain
Nothing you could call fresh, nothing worn down
     Which is fine
I lightly hum a tune
I set wind chimes jangling
But the birds and marmots sleep through it
Nowhere a note in response

December 24, 2010

BAGPIPE

I have a bagpipe but have never blown it
When wind stirs, it moans aloud on its own
No rhythm or melody to speak of
This is probably what some call "the voice of the wind"
In lonely hours, it looks dark red and slender under a lamp
At a gallop, it's icy like a horseman's sharp sword
This is my bagpipe I've never blown
Within it lies the final secret of the universe
I vow not to lose it for a thousand years
Shepherds of any century will not go astray
I rise at dawn one day, slide it over my palm
Then speak these words:
Well then . . . let us walk to the ends of the earth

December 24, 2010

PAIN OF GOING BAREFOOT

Crossing a mountain stream, barefoot in numbing cold
This is late autumn frost, transformed into water
I quiet my mind and wade slowly on the streambed
Thinking how the world always flows like this
The pressure of pebbles underfoot is a familiar pain
Go on walking, let pain rise from the depths of my heart
Let sound fade away, beginning from the soles of my feet
In fact, to cry out in pain would have little meaning
I'm a rover and fond of strong sensations
I'm a rover and fond of boundless spaces
Pausing a while, I upend a stone with my foot
Suddenly it shows a star-flecked spectrum
Making no sound, it rolls with the current
Perhaps it had been wishing for change

December 24, 2010

CROW

I watch a crow pecking beneath leaves for ground bugs
Its sharp claws turn over every leaf
With a tough look in its eyes, it throws pinecones aside
Pecking where it pleases, as if it owns the world
Those dry yellow leaves are ready to become mulch
Those bugs would die by winter anyway
It doesn't fly but only paces the lawn
Clearly its attitude is disdainful of the world
Ceasing its steps, it looks slantwise at everything
Its feathers lie flat to keep out the slightest ray of light
Following it, I'm like one who has lost his way
But I discover nothing amid tufts of grass
I raise a leafy twig to my eyes to inspect it
Crow is not impressed . . . it calmly keeps an eye on me

December 24, 2010

QUIET

In the woods . . . wishing bell sounds carried this far,
Moved with mysterious strides through the foliage
When I gaze up at gleams of light on pinecones
They're always putting on skins of sunlight or starlight
Their moisture carries a scent of bracing cold
Take one step and leave a watermark in the dew
A gay butterfly, eyes closed, sleeps hidden behind leaves
He seems to have squeezed out a few teardrops in dreams
All things look like a young girl who just finished weeping
All things look like a girl's tousled hair after bathing
Be quiet . . . all things may begin to sing in harmony
Be quiet . . . all things may never make a sound again
Glumly I lift my head and stare at the silent trees
Their tossing branches shake down a shower of dew

December 24, 2010

THE BAT'S EARRING

Rainy night . . . a bat flies out from the foliage
It flies around a tree as if seeking its earring
There is an earring glittering in my hand
Raising it skyward, the dark sky seems a shade lighter
A flurry of bats swoops like a nighttime cloud
Or like galloping horses that have shaken off their loads
Once they withdraw into night I begin moving
On a rainy night I can tread quite lightly
I reach out to touch any falling leaf within reach
I expel hot breath, give what warmth I can to the leaves
On a rainy, starless night I seek a clear view of myself
With each step I find a new refuge in the world
I strew a handful of leaves and flowers at the night sky
Whereupon each bat flying through it wears an earring

December 24, 2010

DANCER

On the river bank, a dancer pounds a drum and dances
His campfire leaps up awhile, then dies down
He bounds up from rocky ground then quickly falls to earth
His arms' dancing movements are like someone shucking corn
He's like a fish that glides through churning currents
Facing the flames, he pounds out a rhythm
Bounds about like a pebble on that bare bank
His drumbeat is like an echo emerging from the earth
The drum-pounding dancer does his solitary dance
That spot of fire at the river's edge will die away
I quietly walk over to keep the dancer company
I'm willing to be the onlooker of the century
As I thank him with rhythmic claps of my hands
The dancer makes a deep bow to the fire

December 24, 2010

PASSING THROUGH THE WORLD
ON THE WAY HOME

I quietly walk through the woods, hoping to hear something
Leaves tremble like little birds that want to fly away
The sun—or maybe it's the moon—shines with tender affection
As it passes through foliage, letting me take in its rays
All is calm and quiet, including my soul
I walk quietly, passing through the world on my way home
I see how slowly a little snail crawls along
But that doesn't make me want to outrace him
When I cannot tell dripping dew from falling tears
My only wish is to walk quietly through my passing years
I'm fond of all things, afraid of everything
So I often draw back in my snail shell and stay put
All it takes is a katydid's drone or a dove's coo
And again, I'll accept any person or thing with open arms
 A fairy maiden, for instance, or a little deer

December 27, 2010; Kashgar Hotel

LITTLE STONE

I know this little stone has rolled along the streambed
More durable than a clam, it has never stopped
Viewed through ripples, it seems to have just finished singing
A molly just now polished its scales on its surface
Its outline is visible underwater as it darts about
Nosing and nibbling the stone with its tiny teeth
In times of stillness, the stone is like some days I've spent
Using green moss to hide its presence in the world
Propelled by invisible limbs, a crayfish bumps against the stone
I bend down and see my face reflected in the water
It's weary and weathered like the stone
Eyes blinking, it seems to smile ruefully
But I'd rather believe it is showing tolerance
Tolerant of water . . . tolerant of stones

December 3, 2010; Kashgar Hotel

A BIRD'S FEATHER

What bird shed that colorful feather in mid-air?
It drifts down like a "Twitter" message from deep in the sky
I figure there's no need to gawk and wait expectantly
I've never been one who simply runs into great luck
I'd rather see it land on a little deer
Let her go through the world dressed in a colorful cape
Or maybe it can drift into a young girl's eye
To make the world in her mind's eye forever splendid
But in one gust, the feather is suddenly gone without a trace
Was it caught in an eagle's beak, taken back to line a nest
Where eggs are being brooded to hatch new lives?
That will be fine . . . it will add something to their feathers
Not being a bird, I have nothing to pluck from myself
I can give the world nothing and I owe it nothing
I can only say "I'm sorry" to fawns and young girls

December 27, 2010; Kashgar Hotel

RAIN CAPE

In the rain, a fisherman gave me a rain cape
In truth, I have no wish to avoid rain or cover myself
I want to stand in a row with cormorants, facing the water
With water soaking my back as fish glide by beneath
Second by second, let long chunks of time pass
Letting rain run its course, not minding a single drop
This is the perfect time to put on that rain cape
Thus I want to thank the fisherman and the cormorants
As wisps of white rise from the surface, all turns misty
This is the right time for fish to rise and spit bubbles
As those drowsy cormorants' bodies sway slightly
they dig their sharp talons into the boat's gunwale
I listen to faint bird calls in the forest
I open my hand to watch the rain pooling in my palm
When it crosses my mind to let the cormorants fly away
The rain stops . . . the cormorants dive with open beaks

December 29, 2010

THOUSAND-MILE DESERT

In the vast desert, I walk alone with no thought of position
Meeting with one scorpion after another, I see little difference
Holding their tails erect to flaunt their poisonous barbs
Under sunlight they look like a series of imps
There are no footprints, no camel bells in this vast desert
Wind no sooner stirs than it hides itself in sand
Eyes peer and ache, not knowing what to gaze at
Like myself, not getting a clear fix on things of this world
If only a golden camel would come striding through this wasteland
Heavy breath from its nostrils would moisten my face and eyes
That way after sunset I wouldn't fret over time's passage
I'd close each imaginary door of the night-time desert
It's no use saying "We seem to have met" to scorpions
They trail behind, making camp in my footprints
At last, I stand still, becoming part of the desert
I've passed through its five-hundred-mile expanse

December 29, 2010

FIGMENTS

Midnight . . . deep among snowflakes, a voice calls
No telling if it belongs to a gray rabbit or a dove
Careful gazing on all sides discovers no footprints
So there's no way to decide which way I should go
Flake after flake drifts down as if from the sky's far reaches
Like far travelers looking weary but still eager
I wish to caress all things, but they all stay away
From deep within snowflakes come beckoning sounds
Anything could be in there . . . I reach and feel a pinprick chill
For an instant it allows me to measure the world's warmth
I smile but no response comes from the flake's depths
I imagine someone standing there, bundled in a scarf
She expels breath into a distance that turns crystal clear
Only in stillness can one judge the positions of stars
Gaze for a century . . . still no sight of the cosmic end
Raising my hand to point somewhere on a whim
A snowflake coalesces . . . all things turn to figments

January 4, 2011, Changhewan, Beijing

EMPTY STILLNESS

Under starlight I watch a bat flying back and forth
Being soundless it appears terribly eerie
I breathe lightly to keep from raising the bat's concern
I'd prefer to stand quietly in this world
When I think of snapping my fingers I curse myself
I'd prefer to watch this bat fly back and forth
I slowly lower my eyelids and doze under the stars
Not really weary, not really alert
This is the bat's moment, and I need not clear my throat
Loosening my collar lets my flesh feel the night's frost
Like a white horse that twitches its hind leg
I can walk or not walk, or keep doing whatever I was
As for the bat, I lost track in starlight and wonder
I fear to face empty stillness with nothing intervening
Seeing a flicker of starlight, I know the bat is not far off
It sees me wearing the heavy fetters of solid ground
Yet as emptiness yawns fearsomely around me
Under starlight my arms spread and like a bat I take flight

January 4, 2011, Changhewan, Beijing

28

MARKS OF PASSING TIME

As I search for a clutch of mushrooms
The mountain wind rustles in unfallen leaves
All things give voice as moonlight tilts and pours
I walk windward, heedlessly startling tree frogs and sparrows
Simply waiting . . . that's the feature of this block of time
Just go on walking . . . you'll come to the world's edge
Often while seeking mushrooms, you forget the road home
Mainly from failing to mark your path with piss like a dog
Endlessly forking woodland paths are as puzzling as thought
I could stand a hundred years unable to take a step
Along with a leaf this moonlit night drifts five hundred miles
All the while the hubbub of cries from the world doesn't cease
Picking mushrooms, I hold them up to starlight for a look
Nameless red and white flowers bloom under the moon
I make no claim, not concerned with things beyond mushrooms
Just hunting mushrooms . . . I head for the woods
      and play my own game

January 4, 2011, Changhewan, Beijing

A BOAR'S NIGHT

I follow a boar into the jungle
It rubs against every tree to leave marks for me
It doesn't care if I exist or if leaves fall in front of it
It doesn't think of me as some kind of guest
Through foliage, you sometimes see sunlight, sometimes moonlight
Some thickets have large trees, others have small trees
Quietly observing the boar, at times I wish to rush to it
       and embrace it
Moving about without a fuss, it makes itself at home
It gobbles mushrooms, causing it to exude a musky scent
Like a fig in a tree, it appears and fades amid shafts of light
It seems to be without hope, never raising its head to view the moon
I follow it closely, as if following a tour guide through the century
I sit in moonlight, letting tendrils grow profusely from my hands
I'm no hunter, no more than I'm a teller of secrets
Shielding my eyes with my hands, I push on through the jungle
Because I like this kind of boar and this kind of night

January 4, 2011; Changhewan, Beijing

A FISH BENEATH A LEAF

A little fish hides and treads water beneath a fallen leaf
In fact, it intends to catch a water bug
Its burnished torso reminds me of a vanished dream
It's a mere sliver of my dream's distinct imprint
As the sun edges closer, it pauses in the flow of time
With a downward plunge it's gone, taking the leaf with it
I imagine it underwater, with pursed lips and lashing tail
Thus the world is tossed about ceaselessly in the stream of years
As I sweep my hand over the river, it all disappears
Afterglow hangs in the sky; I see it extending in streaks
Untraceable birds whistle in long sentences
Slowly my shadow takes leave of me in the river
Thrashing as it swims, it seems like a fish grown old
As I look around for a rosewood leaf to cover it
I discover that I've been buried deeply, leaf upon leaf

January 4, 2011; Changhewan, Beijing

WITHIN THE ULTIMATE SECRET

As wind gradually stirs, the night seems to insinuate itself
       into all corners
Through patches of cloud in the cellophane sky, some stars fade
       and some show warmly
You walk within this, aware that plunging into an abyss
       would not be natural
Your heart pounds as if in opposition to the world
Night is still . . . I hear sounds from the distant ocean
At such a moment, no bird or rabbit will pop into view
They may be fast asleep, or staring at me from under cover
I walk along like a taxiing plane or a superfluous object
In the darkness I grab a tree as anchor, to help me stop mid-ocean
Then the tree, taking me as anchor, puts down roots
       in the wasteland
On its leaves I see starlight broken into fragments
Rabbit and bird are wide-eyed, as if discussing the ultimate secret
My clothes are wet . . . I cup my hands to make a lantern
I hoped it would light up sky and earth, but it only shines
       three meters
Wind gradually lifts me, blows me toward another destination

January 11, 2011; Changhewan, Beijing

ONE WHO CARRIES A RIFLE

I'm one who carries a rifle as I walk along edges of fields
With nothing to do, it's my habit to walk on criss-cross paths
When wheat kernels fall, I know it's the world's way of speaking
Or that the kernels are provisions left out for sparrows
Innocuous clouds float in puffs, until it's hard to be aware of them
Wherever I point my gun, stillness stretches out before me
When wind blows, meek and slender wheat stalks fall over
It's time for them to become a blanket for field mice
Under such conditions I become a big strapping fellow
Carrying a rifle and sweeping my eyes over the world
When I roar, it's enough to cause a storm
Which stirs up the desire for mastery over anyone I see
Wondering if this is an illusion, I tramp on my own shadow
It doesn't say much and won't move a single step away
I turn my back on the sun to prove my distance from the world
My shadow walks ahead of me shouldering a rifle

January 11, 2015

TELLER OF SECRETS

As I walk into the forest, a shadow of some kind streaks by me
Then the foliage tosses about and settles as if congealed in oil
      paint
At this point I'd rather believe the shadow is still flying
Like a teller of secrets that has stumbled into God's private affairs
A tree frog holds its breath, getting ready for a trans-century leap
So I know it's not part of that shadow
The trees interlock their fingers under mulch and moss
Clearly they see me as some kind of interloper
Every place I go a hush gathers around me
Making me suspect that deep down I could be a tree
Such an identity ensures that I'll never become an arsonist
Or will never be the one who gets lost in a forest
I need only to turn about and vanish behind a tree
Noontime rays shine on beads of sweat in the palm of my hand
Pursing my lips I whistle into the forest's depths
Then wait for a horse to come galloping this way

January 11, 2011; Changhewan, Beijing

THE DOVE'S OWNER

Along with a feather, I come to rest on the ground
It's a talisman left by the dove I let out to fly
Whether it will fly back is a world-class riddle
Whether it exists is a topic worth delving into
The feather whirls over tips of grass . . .
       thus grass shows splendid colors
I rejoice in being a lucky observer
As the feather skims over rock, a butterfly takes it for a sail
It latches onto the feather, thinking it will soar to far reaches
       of the cosmos
After the butterfly flies away, the feather lands on a horse's back
This moment one imagines it transforming into an unrivaled
       princess
She ambles along, unconcerned with the passage of time
       or with daily life
She drinks wine, combs her hair, and waits for her lover's letters
Such earthshaking matters pertain to a feather in the afternoon
Thus I sense something affectionate about this world
As owner I raise the feather into air, letting the sun's rays light it
The dove returns, carries off the feather and is gone without a trace

January 11, 2015; Changhewan, Beijing

THE BLUENESS OF AN IRIS

I can never figure out the mystery of an iris' blooming
Its pale violet or deep blue makes me feel part of time's passage
Before dewfall I start to observe their crystalline color
And wonder if there is a rueful ache bound up in it
Just think how it's trodden down by camels in the vast desert
Even vipers like to entwine themselves around its stalk
As for me I like to sleep next to it with my clothes on
Roused by the clank of camel bells at dawn, I will sit up
Nothing I do has any relation to the blooming of an iris
In fact the iris' display is probably all for naught
Irises are seen everywhere, even on desolate sand flats and dunes
When I venture to the sky's edge, it exudes that same scent
It proliferates so excessively you can't be bothered to pick it
Clanking camel bells tell me it's time to shake off dewdrops
I neither wish nor need to wear a disguise in front of my
        companions
With that deep purple adrift under the starry sky . . .
        I'll close my eyes

January 11, 2011; Changhewan, Beijing

EARLY WINTER SNOW

Someone is walking on the snow, light and easy, leaving no trace
Yet a flock of tiny birds seems to fly up, beating gold-feathered wings
Out of snow-mist they drop and plunge into a snowdrift
And the world has an interval of spotless, crystalline repose
This is early winter snow, so it's moist and fluffy
One can even catch its breath-like scent, faint and warm
A palm pressed deep into snow is free from fear of jagged edges
Take a long look . . .refraction of sun on snow sends out
      eye-catching beams
You'll start to think of yourself as a black-eyed, red-lipped fox
Crouch low with closed eyes, wait for weariness to steal up
On snowy ground, you see things far away, hear sounds distinctly
Just think, this snow may have sifted down from your ancestors'
      era
When your grandpa's grandpa took an axe to a thousand-year-old
      cedar tree
Wave in any direction on snowy ground and you can greet your
      forefathers
Across snowy ground you drag your snowy-white comings
      and goings
Stepping gingerly to leave no tracks, not turning to look back

January 16, 2011; Changhewan, Beijing

GRANDMA

Grandma sits asleep under a wisteria vine
Like an old cat tranquilly wheezing
In noon sun, she's like a fall gourd hanging down
Withered yellow with no scent of growth
No more will her dreams fly like butterflies
She's just an old woman counting the days
She no longer gets roused up by the planting of any seed
Harvest really has nothing to do with her
As things are, light just flares up and dies down
Grandma is like a dozing cat with ears laid back
Even mice forage carelessly by her toes
Always finding rice that fell through Grandma's teeth
In autumn the wind makes things clink and rustle
But Grandma's eyes are tightly closed
Her ears are solidly plugged up
Waipo is dead to the world

January 19, 2011; Changhewan, Beijing

DRIED-UP WATER LILIES IN WINTER

A winter's day . . . a few ravaged water lilies stand half-erect on the
    icy pond
Like abandoned children of sunlight they hunch over, meek and
    hopeless
I try hugging my body tightly, not feeling the slightest warmth
All through the sun's east-to-west course, my heart remains icy
I think of those little carp beneath ice, still puffing their cheeks
I've watched a thousand suns pass over a thousand ponds
An offhand caress or glancing touch never does any good
Those thousand suns just slid past the ice, leaving no trace
I walk over the ice to let the fish know I'm here
The sunlight leaves me totally unmoved
There's nothing that can tie it to memories of summer
Ah, balm of tender greenness . . . that was a different kind of sun
Reaching out, as easy as you please, to embrace this world
And the world, for its part, illumined the thousand suns
Standing firmly, I give the sun a wide-eyed look
A winter's day . . . I know the frigid stiffness of dried-out
    water lilies

January 21, 2011; Changhewan, Beijing

MOTHER RABBIT IN A DESERTED CAVE

As an early riser . . . take a nice, slow morning walk
Not touched by greatness, you can walk along at ease
Even sparrows are still sleeping, due to the bitter icy wind
Once wind sets in, this world and daily life start to seem dreary
Watching the sky brighten, like layers of gauzy curtains pulled
    open
I undo button after button, opening my chest to the air
Suddenly I realize I'm not truly steadfast or beautiful after all
Under the light, I look weather-beaten and fatigued
This really is a morning when early rising is of no use
I tread on dry leaves, leaving unaccountable footprints
Guessing where the sun will rise, I turn my steps that way
At any rate, I still have a pair of bright eyes
My gaze can penetrate the night's darkness
I can see to the bottom of things with ease
For instance, now I see a mother rabbit in a deserted cave
With her hot red tongue, she's licking her children

January 21, 2011; Changhewan, Beijing

TRAIN PLATFORM IN AUTUMN

I no longer wish to await someone or send someone off
Yet I wish to stand on the platform in autumn and listen to trains
Gazing at that familiar distant view, I'll watch as a train draws
      near then pulls away
The past is like a loaded railroad car, heavy and no longer related
      to me
Three hundred steps to the east is the spot where I embraced a girl
      in tears
Three hundred steps west is the occasion when I parted forever
      from a girl
It's all unfamiliar now, yet one comes across it anywhere
Leading a camel, I travel to and fro through my country
Like puffs of smoke, my emotions roar to life then dissolve into
      stillness
Tree leaves no sooner fall in decay than new green appears
      on branches
Gray magpies hardly finish molting before they get busy having
      children
In fact, I've never been able to tell which is daddy and which
      grandpa
The conductress no longer blows a whistle, so she no longer seems
      impressive
While saluting, she keeps an eye on her past selves whizzing by
      in the windows
She has become just anyone and has no connection to anyone
Of course, she's someone whom I never awaited nor sent off
The distant view turns bleak when I think of it as encountering
      a century
Raising my arm, I think I should salute my future and my past

January 23, 2011; Changhewan, Beijing

MOUNTAIN RANGE

After autumn winds . . . off in the distance a mountain range shows
    its outline
One can imagine countless birds chirping and squawking there
I'm amazed that I never paid attention to that range before
That's like remaining unaware of responsibilities I bear in daily
    life
In those mountains, there must be leaves drifting in the wind
After lighting each bird nest in turn, the setting sun leaves them
    in darkness
Due to eating too much or chirping too hard, the birds have
    gone to sleep
By now, a poetic stillness must have settled over that mountain
    range
I stand beneath the afterglow, intently scanning those mountains
    at twilight
Figuring my distance from that range and its relation to me
In doing so, I discover that I actually stand at the world's center
I murmur . . . I grieve . . . I watch every move I make
As I raise my hand toward the mountain range, I find it has
    disappeared
Sky and land merge in obscurity . . . the moon slowly rises
I let the quarrels of birds replay itself in my ears
As I allow tears to run down my cheeks
After autumn wind comes dark night . . . no time for a clear
    view of anything
No time to get a look at my countenance in the mirror

January 28, 2011; Changhewan, Beijing

42

MOURNFUL NOTES IN A FOREST

Beneath willow branches, I quiet down and listen to sounds
    of living things
I want to hear the low-toned frogs sing counterpoint to high
    cicadas
Both show interest in fallen leaves and like to nestle among them
As for me . . . nothing much can move me, so I remain unfazed
In the woods, hoof beats approach from afar, then head back
    into the distance
Sparrows fly up in small flocks then drop earthward again
These are everyday things in the world of appearances
As for me . . . I don't take much interest and so I'm indifferent
A dove walks along a path instead of flying
It doesn't look injured but cannot flap its wings
Perhaps it ran away from its flock and is heading off to die
As for me . . . I don't grieve much, so I don't say a word
Another dove lands in a treetop and perches to watch
It makes no sound, doesn't make the slightest move
As for me . . . I don't have many words, so this is hard to express
Watching the doves I hear mournful notes in the forest

January 21, 2011; Zhongkun Building

A BIG RIVER

I see a big river move sluggishly, its current rolling in the sunlight
In fact, the setting sun can only light the water three feet down
It resembles my grandfather, raising his hand languidly
Blocking the phlegm of his cough as the dike blocks the surge of
      water
I hardly expect the sunlight to warm up that massive flow of water
That's why it looks a little bleak . . . gloomy and unfathomable
As a sparrow flies over the surface, I feel a tightening in my back
I worry that a whitecap will knock it out of the air, swallowing its
      remains
The big shimmering river is like a subdued echo of the cosmos
It gives me an urge to recite some kind of epic, to tell stories
But I definitely lack the gall to throw even a broken pebble at it
I think . . . we are magnificent in our servitude and must not resist
I fear the big river will disappear, without warning, at the horizon
I'm oversensitive, yet long-accustomed to insignificance
      and inferiority
I watch the big river heave and turn over without a sound
Like a mighty father hiding his open hand behind his back

January 23, 2011; Zhongkun Building

44

A MAN HUNTING FOR STONES

I'm a tranquil person and thus accustomed to hunting stones in
    the wasteland
On moonlit nights they eye me coldly; at sunset their gleam
    is beyond fathoming
I walk as lightly as a cat, trying hard not to bump into things
Stones in the wasteland are numerous, showing that all things have
    fragile beauty
Just because I lack feathers doesn't mean I harbor a wish to fly
I want to see the metallic stone that streaked earthward in last
    night's dream
Yet tonight there's a sky full of meteors dropping onto the wasteland
Who can tell if this is an omen of death or a symbol of new life?
I'd rather await a wolf to proclaim they have nothing to do with him
He has no ties of feeling or karma with any stone
It's a night of magnificent beauty, of too great a disparity with me
In the human wasteland I'm only a person who hunts stones
When I strike sparks from flint, I only wish to start a cooking fire
But I've become a pursuer of wolves, setting fires on all sides
I stand in the wasteland piling up a cairn of stones
Beginning with this, the world becomes a cairn of mani stones

January 30, 2011; Changhewan, Beijing

SUSPIRATIONS OF THE COSMOS

An empty night . . . I sit up and listen to suspirations from across
     the cosmos
What a joy to hear a chord with such unhurried, even tones
Deep down in darkness its many-veined arabesques come rippling
Perhaps this is a prelude to a season of bountiful rain on earth
I grab one hand with the other, to keep from crying out
     in amazement
I think I really must learn how to be a citizen of the cosmos
That is, no matter how ugly and vile I discover myself to be
I still want to believe it will come to a wonderful end
In fact, this syndrome typifies a good fellow of the world
To eat my own fingers or other people's is not a matter of evil
When a layered aurora hangs in the air, trees will shed their leaves
It will be a sere and golden world, fragmented yet covered in beauty
As for me, I want to run jingling across hills and rivers,
     acting as God's bell
Ringing a melody I devised to resonate with the other side
     of the cosmos
I no longer daub out my feelings in red or black ink
I merely lie still in a certain corner of this universe
I wave at someone in the starry sky, draw the curtains
Then go back to the bedroom and sleep

January 31, 2015; Changhewan, Beijing

WHEAT SPROUTS UNDER SNOW

Seeing the wheat sprouts asleep under snow makes me feel weary
Due to the dry spell, their quilt is looking threadbare this year
Yet my fondest wish is to stay in bed all through this century
I fear aging . . . I fear change . . . worst of all I fear no one will like me
Wheat plants feel safe just smelling each other's scent
Another advantage is that sparrows and bugs can't hatch their
       broods in time
Such humdrum, threadbare snow after Lunar New Year
       makes all things look off kilter
To be sure, no one will die of thirst . . . we'll get through
       these dreary months
Here beneath the sun I cannot bear to take steps and leave footprints
Being doubtful and full of trepidations, I vacillate
This stretch of snow is for wheat plants . . . they need someone to
       watch over it
It's like when you write a line of poetry quietly
       and don't have to read it aloud
Imagining that a big snowfall will blanket the earth tomorrow
I tell myself no one will howl again from a cold that keeps them
       awake
Opening my window, I gaze past willow trees toward tomorrow
       evening
As for now, I might as well cross my legs and sit up straight in bed

February 22, 2015; Los Angeles

MY SISTER'S MOONLIGHT

An oak tree motionless in a yard thousands of miles from home
The squirrel is probably sleeping like nobody's business
Oblivious to which pine cone or leaf pillows his head
And yet starlight probably still peeks through the oak tree
So it looks like a cloth-shaded lantern with the light down low
It sequesters the light within itself and lets it out in beams
Like my big sister tucking covers around her little brothers
      and sisters at night
This moment . . . Sister has let her hair down; she is half-awake
      and half-dreaming
As her arm reaches out, she gives off a hint of tree scent
Thousands of miles away, I rise from sleep . . . I'm by no means an
      uninvited guest
I'm the owner of an oak tree, and I'd never do anything to hurt it
I have no idea how many leaves it has lost, how many new leaves
      it has grown
I've never looked into how many generations of Mr. Squirrel
      have climbed it
Thousands of miles from home . . . when it stops moving, that's
      enough to concern me
For its sake, I fly back and forth, repeatedly reciting
      the lines of a poem

February 22, 2011; Los Angeles

WALKING WITHIN SOUND

I've been wanting to walk within sound . . . to pass through a forest
      or the world
But late at night when stars are screened off by clouds, the whole
      place has an end-of-the world look
No way to hear or imagine the moans of azaleas as they bloom
Or purple chrysanthemums as they face the bracing air of autumn
On gorgeous sunny days all living things are probably cheering
When carp leap from the surface maybe they are whistling
After dark, my grandma would stop burping to listen for a knock
She was waiting for grandpa to return from another world
When a plane flies overhead I think of people who come from
      beyond the horizon
They drink milk, eat corn, and come to shop at Zhongkun Square
      near Big Bell Temple
Honeybees would never bang repeatedly on gongs or yell loudly
Ten thousand years ago they tuned themselves to a certain key
      for the sake of this world
Walking within sound, I'm like a flower in full bloom or a piece
      of rusting iron
Even so, I do my best to slow down my heartbeat
Before laying blame or cursing, I should sit awhile at a field's edge
Like a cricket and vibrate tiny hairs to make this world tranquil

February 22, 2011; Los Angeles

49

A TRAIN IN THE OCEAN

At dawn's first light, a train makes a sound in the ocean
In truth, I know this happens because I came to live beside the sea
Where I imagine iron wheels speeding through the brine
I have ln't ridden on it nor gazed out its windows
At this moment the ocean's vast darkness makes for a deep stillness
Fish are asleep at different depths
Fearing a chill, I dare not lie stargazing on the surface
Thus I'm not likely to be crushed flat by a train
I'm eager for light to shine on the sea so I can discern people
        behind the windows
Among them I suppose there will be a messenger from another
        cosmos
Aside from this, I hope a blacktip reef shark will breach the surface
The slender grace of its muscular curves will look like a sprout
        in the sea
I also like to soak my feet in seawater to get a taste of being a fish
Of course I'll never become a passenger on that train
It won't happen . . . this is my time to say goodbye to everything
I quiet down, perk my ears and listen for cold tremors in steel rails

February 22, 2011; Los Angeles

50

THE GREEN SNAKE SHEDS ITS SKIN

For a long time I forgot to view the moon
Like a green snake that forgot to shed its skin
As that notion occurs to me, I hear the clank of camel bells
Thick doors and windows cannot hold back its penetrating force
I think this must be due to the brightness of tonight's moon
I interlock my fingers in the shape of iris petals
Tonight's moon glistens wet and warm, perfect for making all
      things grow
Even an old root, parched and soil-colored, is quite likely to send
      out sprouts
Viewing the moon, you can firmly believe that a new era is coming
You also believe a caravan is striding beneath the ancient desert
And one thousand meters below that, a big river still surges
As one who forgot the moon, I can't help but feel unworthy
I think this may be why I neglect certain points of etiquette
I don't care about shiny white hairs standing like stingers on my head
I think this is what a forgetter of moonlight deserves
Now that I've jumped like a frog across a stream
I start to get accustomed to sitting in the moon's shadow

February 22, 2011; Los Angeles

A PINK CLOUD OF PINE-SCENT

In morning light, a squirrel awakens . . . its scampering rustles
     in the pine needles
Pine scent diffuses into the air . . . downwind it makes a plume
     of pinkish scent
The squirrel slides down, bending needles to the grass,
     then goes to find water
It's looking for crystal-green dewdrops swaying on leaves
I realize it would be useless to greet it . . . I'm a stranger here
In this world, I'm just another kind of leaf
I never stay by one tree too long to avoid getting entrenched
Even dark nights may be my time to drift about in the world
Some leaves take in light that turns them to stars, and they grow
Day by day along with their tree, but this isn't my lot in life
Thus I maintain ample distance from any one star
Imagining that I too could grow a squirrel-like tail makes me laugh
     to myself
If that happened, I'd take a nice hundred-year nap in an oak tree
Moonlight and sunlight would shine on me, letting me grow a
     thousand-layer metal skin
Even then, I'd only be an extraordinary acorn in an oak tree
When the little squirrel slept with arms around me,
     I'd share my warmth
Then lie with eyes wide open while cicadas drone in the long night

February 23, 2011; Los Angeles

AN EAGLE ENTERS MY DREAM

Backlit by sunset, the line of the lakeshore is misty as a young
      girl's line of sight
I persuade myself that an eagle just now took cover among trees
      and grasses
It sailed along like a leaf without effort, then dropped out of sight
      in a blink
From an unseen source comes the clinking of pendants
      on someone's waist
I proceed fishlike along the lake's shore to get a sense of a fish's
      tranquility
Now my parched lips have been moistened; they are finely-shaped
      like leaves of a lakeside willow
I think of that eagle serenely closing its round eyes
Drowsiness like a ring of ripples expands into the mind's depths
In the water there is no shadow of me, no moon, no stars
Neither fish nor frogs jump in—*kerplunk*—and hop out
When I suspect all of this to be an illusion, I begin to hesitate
I'd rather my heart be wracked by pain than be someone
      of no consequence
I pass my fingers through the water, not sensing its iciness
      and clarity
Maybe leaves and eagles never cared much about such things
Now that an eagle has entered my dream, I should get some sleep
Lie down fully clothed and sleep by the lake

February 24, 2011; Los Angeles

53

REMNANT STARLIGHT

In the light of dawn, there are birdcalls and remnant light
  from a few stars
Being in an alien land, I can't discern the types of birds
  nor the mood of their cries
I look carefully into each clump of leaves but only see quick stirrings
When desire arises like a pinecone swaying on a branch tip,
  I close my eyes
In this lifetime, I've never exuded a fresh scent like those
  pinecones or needles
For many years I've stood silently at windows watching how
  the sky brightens
And how the first butterfly flits into my field of vision
But that calling bird never allows me to come face to face with it
At each call, I feel like swooning from the unworthiness I feel
  in my heart
I cannot make out the differences between bird calls in summer
  and in fall
I cannot tell if they are mature or if they are slowly getting old
Each time her presence is veiled on a branch tip, the world around
  her is hushed
Fragile helplessness clings like a leaf to a tree and won't let go
The sun rises but the tree remains in mist
Sunlight like a golden cloth screens off all the affairs of the world

February 25, 2011; Los Angeles

BAMBOO HUT

I've been looking for a little bamboo hut in the forest
All traces of it are lost amid the thick foliage
I recall that a boar once snuck in and ate yams left near the stove
Little green snakes come each year to shed their skins under its eaves
Walking among scents of greenery I often wish to hide behind any
      nearby tree
One could say that the world's relation to me is that of a screen
When dew condenses thick as rain, I raise my head
I look forward to resting my eyes on a beetle crawling down
      the trunk
Its gorgeous spots of color are like a diagram of celestial movements
It looks like a daughter coming home after receiving blessings from
      heaven
This moment, I wish to pass like a deer through highland forests
      and this world
While searching for that old, weathered hut that's mottled with
      streaks of green
Leave time for light to show through in the sky . . . let mountain
      wind stroke my face
Like one who has lost his way but is in no hurry to take
      the homeward route
Neither roused nor dejected when falling leaves fill the sky
Walking in highland forests, trying to emerge from this world's
      forbidden zone

February 25, 2011; Los Angeles

OBSERVER OF THE WORLD

A bird stands in a treetop, rocking like a leaf in the wind
I point my finger at it to confirm its existence
In fact, what I want to confirm is my position in this world
Although it's not remotely possible that I'll perch in a tree
I enjoy sunlight shining on my back like when a bird ruffles
     its feathers
Guessing where the bird flies off to, I become an observer
     of the world
When the scents of trees in the air turns pithy, I know fall is near
I'll be like a bird that stops ruffling to keep from falling like a leaf
In this season, the path of moss-covered rip-rap does not tempt
me   to set foot there
I hope a bird will pop its head up from a nest and sing to me
I assume a pose of waiting for time to grow old
A bird can fly for a thousand miles, a thousand years, and no one
     worries about the course it takes
To stand in a treetop and survey all things is to be like a bird
     or a leaf
Wherever a finger points . . . that place waits like a secret passageway
After daybreak, I take my time under the sun,
     coughing decisively and loudly
A bird flies up and disappears over the far horizon

February 25, 2011; Los Angeles

THE SEA LION'S CHILD

After a day in the sunlight, gulls congregate like a herd of horses
Standing on the deck or on spars, each looks into the distance
      like a figurehead
Because the sea is not rangeland, no sounds of galloping are heard
I'd like to know how the mother sea lion cuddles with her
      children after dark
When her hoarse voice proclaims that she is mother to the world
I prepare to pass fishlike through this lagoon into another oceanic
      expanse
Ssunlight has baked me to the texture of glittering fish scales
Seawater is so bracing that my skin tightens, and my mind as well
I search intently for reasons why fish would jump above the surface
High tide and ebb tide don't enter into my moods
I merely wish to face the sea and breathe with open mouth
      like any fish
I cannot blow bubbles or sweep my gleaming silver tail
But I delight in how sunlight warms the sea and the sailboats on it
Aside from the lapping of tidewater, I no longer hear any sound
And think that this may be an indication that I've gone over
      to the fishy side

February 26, 2011; Newport Beach

DISTANCE FROM THE WORLD

Late at night, I sit at the seaside pondering the question
      of distance from this world
And I force myself to observe how far reflected stars can drift
      on the sea's surface
Now that the stars have changed to fish swarming homeward
      from afar, I'm at a loss
I would rather the stars change to little mums planted all over the sea
There are endless discussions of singing and recitation, but I can't
      hear a thing
Apparently, here in the darkness I'm truly one of the blind
Thank heaven for the waves . . . bit by bit they bring me a feeling
      of coolness
Opening my mouth, I let the ocean breeze pass through my body
Recalling my treks through deserts, my climbs up steep paths,
      I almost dive into the sea
I need someone to embrace me tightly, as if in a mother's arms
Seashells on the shore are like dry leaves being tossed about
      by waves
They were once stars of the sea; now they no longer give off light
A beached fish leaps about, but no seagull comes to devour it
There is only a line of footprints heading straight for the ocean's
      depths
By the arrangement of stars, I have prepared markers
      for the return trip
Then from the ocean's surface, grows an array of silvery gray
      narcissus

February 26, 2011; Newport Beach

BOAT WITH LOWERED SAILS

At dusk, like a boat with lowered sails, I quiet down and wait
    for what will happen
At last I'm in the mood to observe a spider hanging from a tiny
    filament
I neatly draw a dividing line, in time and light, between past
    and future
When that thread gleams, whistles blare and fade near or far
    in the world
I'm terribly afraid a dragonfly will come as an intruder from
    another realm
I'm aware that it eats bugs, but this one may also grab hold
    of a plump duck
After feeding on the duck, by night it will plant its feathers
    in a little grove
When it severs that spider's thread, the world will suffer a painful
    spasm
I cry out and stomp in consternation, but people watch
    as if nothing has happened
The setting sun, without flouncing even once, radiates its poem
    in bold red as usual
The hollow vault of sky extends straight to the edge of the cosmos
I want to fly up in the air, brandishing a leather whip like a drover
Or be like a giant spider that hangs and swings from the stars
All night looking in the mirror of the moon, brushing its teeth
    and painting its brows
When someone's eyes are puffy with sleep, telling a story
    makes no difference

March 3, 2011; Changhewan, Beijing

SEA BEAST

Expecting a school of water beasts to loom up from the tide, I'm
      gripped by anxiety
I worry that my paranoid fantasies of the sea will become reality
I see the breakers turn white, one by one, then ebb, hurling sand
      at the feet of girls
I feel I may merge into the water as my body grows tail and fins
Yet no one has the courage to raise an outcry or show alarm
The surf rolls in from far away, as if bringing the evil of millennia
Barbarity and self-righteousness of the past have gradually been
      washed away
As waves fall back I no longer think *So that's all there is*
Seeing a mussel in the sunlight slightly opening its shell, I feel
      a pang in my heart
The sea's wiry, dark claws lay hold of a crab trying to crawl ashore
There's no need to explain how I know . . . I'm an inmate
      who won't be making any jailbreaks
The anchor of a sunken ship loops around me to keep me
      from getting out of line
Like a wide-open eye on the sea floor, its all-penetrating vision is
      tormented by sunlight
On the seabed I'll plant purple vetch to feed my seahorses
      and sea sheep
On an alien shore, feeling an urge to tell stories, I take off my
      travel coat
A cold and salty moistness diffuses into the air of the world

March 6, 2011, Dubai

HEADY SCENT OF TREE BLOSSOMS

Tree blossoms that give off heady scent grow dim . . . half facing
    the desert, half facing the sea
It's hard to imagine when they'll close their eyes and sleep
Fruits among leaves stirred by fifty breezes are plundered
    by quick-darting birds, leaving nothing but a vigil
A tree blossom grows succulent in layers, like a tender-hearted
    rabbit
On Dubai beach I raise my arm and beckon into the distance
Then I release my horse to become what it pleases—a tortoise in
    the sea or a snake in the desert
Being a man who will soon return home I roll up my trousers
    and stride along the shore
I amble along with no wish to fly or ruffle my feathers
With bated breath I pluck a flower from the waves
Thus I'm outraged to see the backwash sweep a leaf quickly past me
Due to distance, the open sea's tranquility is an absolute illusion,
    which gives it a gorgeous color
Which makes it absolutely unbelievable that a water beast
is even now hatching five hundred million eggs under the sea
The beast ambles and dozes in warm currents . . .
    sometimes it even eats its progeny
It spits up phlegm and saliva that give off eerie rays of light
At a time like this, to sing any number of country songs would not
    be excessive and deserves to be mentioned
I turn away, feeling revulsion and emotional fatigue

March 6, 2011, Dubai

SEEDS

On a mountain path amid melting snow, many seeds are cracking open
They're like chips of teeth . . . half buried in mud or caught
      between grass blades
These days, warm sunlight slants down at different angles
      over a ridge
In imperceptible stages, seeds launch barely visible threads of green
There are movements in a grove . . . whole patches of undergrowth
      toss about
That must be boars and badgers awakened by my noise, roused
      from hibernation too early
I try my best to step lightly, but the rocks knock against each other
This appears to be a phase when living things are fragile and sensitive
I gaze at far mountains . . . from here their dry foliage gleams like
      filigree in a crown
No birds are seen whirring skyward and no snake comes here
      to shed its skin
As for the seeds, their pods and coats are strewn along the path
      like underwear put out to dry
Just think, those were once the firm outer walls of their worlds,
      safe and warm
That being so, I would like to think that seeds resting
      in a ptarmigan's belly or in the scat of a boar
Before they are transformed into a civet's flesh would much
      rather remain unborn and never see anyone
Opening my hands, I let sunlight and mountain breeze pass
      through my fingers
Because I feel a seed is getting ready to send forth its sprout like that.

March 29, 2011; Beijing

A FRAZZLED FEATHER

I recognize this frazzled feather now lodged among twigs and leaves
While gazing at it last winter, I seemed to hear a ptarmigan's cry
      deep in a thicket
In melting snow, it was like a bright-hued twig from God's
      garden flashing enigmatic rays
Just think of its owner, most likely so beautiful that one could
      not look straight at her
It's hard to say about moonlit nights . . . maybe it became
      an iridescent star and flew away
When it got to Denmark, it was plaited into the mermaid's
      garland, then flew back before dawn
Like when I rode my beloved horse, galloping great distances
      at night just to bathe a narcissus
Aside from this, I cannot sing or play guitar or express
      my emotional state to anyone
It occurs to me that on the afternoon when this feather's vividness
      comes to an end, there will be a snowstorm or rain
Now everything slowly quiets down . . . nothing is tossing about
Realizing that the ptarmigan may not care about any of these
      things, my heart feels a pang, my eyes moisten
In a mountain grove, I breathe in big gasps and take big steps
      like I own the place
Somehow, I should think of a way to give the world a big surprise
Although in reality I never draw attention to myself
      or buttonhole people
Stars destined to be extinguished are falling one by one . . .
      I begin to mutter to myself
At this moment, frost condenses on my eyelashes, cool and crystalline

March 29, 2011; Copenhagen

CURTAIN OF SNOW

Staring at distant peaks through a curtain of snow, I want nothing
        more than to get moving
I've always been tantalized by obscure mistiness and unknown
        prospects
It fascinates me to think that an arctic fox may walk on my trail
With starry eyes and thin red tongue, she discerns wind direction
        and my sad mood
In the snowy season, I feel my soul and body being suffused with light
My hands are milky-hued but warm . . . even covered
        with snowflakes they do not flounce
To my right a polar bear leaves a line of huge footprints, to my left
        sled dogs yelp
As for me, I'm hesitant, and my arctic fox wavers right along
        with me
Behind those far mountains its seems gulls are soaring
        and some kind of beings are raising their cries
Whether you listen, whether you watch has no relation
        to society and shouldn't be held against you
Riding an imaginary white horse or a red yak, I hope to reach
        a secret spot behind that snow curtain
Or etake flight like a bird, high among snowflakes, and be a kite
        within that curtain of snow
While walking in solitude, I become a whale on a long migration
Lost and adrift in the Gulf Stream, I wait days for the sun
        to brighten
When fed up or fatigued, I don't care how many layers of snow
        curtain cover me
This moment, an arctic vixen walks in the curtain of snow . . .
        without anyone knowing, she retracts her claws

April 5, 2011; Arctic Circle

JOURNEY

On a journey, I pass through airports and highway traffic,
    which makes me even more solitary
I see each red cap as a crabtree flower, not caring about nationality
I sit on the floor, back against the wall, listening with closed eyes
I have no nostalgia for a local accent
At this moment, I hold a question and answer session, treating
    myself as my own father or mother or sibling
Making a notepad of my palm, I write down destinations
    and times of departure
I'd rather hide my wristwatch to forget the passing
    of my motherland's years
Sometimes I knock on a door you're not likely to open,
    pretending to be happy to return
But I'm still unwilling to pull out an express ticket home
This is a solitary journey on which I can smile and greet anyone
Even looking in the mirror on impulse doesn't worry me,
    so why should anyone snicker?
Flying in sunlight . . . flying in the starry sky . . . I can survey all
    below me . . . I can look toward higher levels
Like when I walked through scrub land as a child, blowing
    dandelion seeds toward some mysterious place
Like wanting to walk into a rainbow as a child . . .
    a passageway to somewhere without borders
When I know I'm lost, I draw a question mark on the land
    to ask the world
I grab hold of an apple and warm it in my hands so the journey
    won't be too lonely
When it's about to sprout, I come through on another journey
    and eat it up
After that, I'm in front of a fruit stand, buying a pile of apples
    from a young woman

                April 6, 2011; Arctic Circle

A FUGITIVE

I stick my bare feet into the dark night to gauge the temperature
    of starlight or what sort of beings are moving in the distance
Moisture in starlight has unseen rose-scented layers
    which propel me to widen my eyes
The pooch in that little grove isn't barking, maybe because
    the little lynx went off to find colored feathers
At this point you can go anywhere and won't fall into an abyss
    or lose the way back
At this moment white stones can change into tadpoles wiggling
    their tails in the night sky
I suppress my sighs of appreciation to become part of this night
    and this world
Memories of grief and love drift up from the bottom of your mind
On a night like this, anything might deserve being sobbed over
    or copiously wept over in private
The thickness of night is the reason I'm unwilling to speak
    or write about my own secrets or those of others
When I go barefoot, I consider myself a fugitive or a man
    with no shadow
I realize that one autumn day all leaves will fall, dry up, and decay
Thence, blossom scent wafts in the dark night and the starry sky
    is festooned with wisteria
When I discover a ring of mushrooms that sprang up
    overnight in the mist, I don't express amazement
Because that could be a lovebird in its changeable guise,
    growing a new type of wings
I admit that I get into a mood of envious enthrallment
    when I think of the mortal fates of true lovers
But I'm not a lovebird, so I can only go barefoot on a certain
    night and wax misty-eyed under the stars

April 26, 2011; Shigatse, Tibet

66

HALFWAY THROUGH THE NIGHT

As a dog barks, I wonder about the far side of the cosmos
        and the number of its stones
I suddenly wish to walk up a mountain path like a blind man
        into the long night
Whether the moonlight is watery, whether stars wink . . .
        right now these are moot questions
I want only to listen to how the world falls asleep
        and to that sigh deep down in darkness
Tramping along on leaves, I can no longer determine my latitude
        or how lost I might be
In truth, I'd like to wait for an angel to come plucking a harp
The air is so damp that a wild dove doesn't want to flap its wings
        and fly toward the starry sky
Scent of a gardenia bush wafts ten meters into cracks of a rockpile
When I hear the final cries of a nocturnal bird, I know
        I'm halfway through the night
After this, hoof beats will probably come rushing over the landscape
A girl's tears will run down, gleaming in cold rivulets
Faint glowing streaks appear in the woods;
        the pattering of feet sounds like teeth being strewn
When I perk my ears in a certain direction, I hear a dog barking,
        which makes me feel close to living things
I want to open my shirt and warm any beings that are feeling cold,
        even phantoms
As long as frost coats my eyelashes, I'm not concerned with what
        is crystalline and misty in this world
Tapping a dry branch, I wait for a flouncing movement
        in the forest canopy

May 9, 2011; Shigatse, Tibet

67

MERCURY FLOWERS

Mercury flowers float demurely around the pond, like tender flesh
     of the cosmos
As my glance sweeps over them, I blush as if peeking
      at the breasts of a holy woman
Now that clouds have covered things, I listen, amazed, to busy
     hammering all through the world
When cattail fluff from a reed bed starts flying, light from behind
      makes it look like a violet or blue handkerchief
I suppose that fruity scent diffusing through the water comes from
      the sacred fruit just now eaten by a water fox
Three inches underwater, pliant stems of green algae are taken
      into the mouth of a golden fish
Taking a sideways view of ripples I see pairs of grief-stricken eyes
      looming up through the water
The sun shudders, tears run down the stems of reeds,
      moistening everything
Having plucked a thin cane stem, I do not blow on it but just
      warm it in in my fingers
As the little river clam parts its shell everything quietly waits
      for what will protrude
A bullfrog snatches a fallen flower with its pink tongue,
      then goes back into its cave
I sit as the sun passes above, waiting for the holy woman to come
     to wash and comb her hair
Even in the dark night, I wish to absorb moisture and stimuli
      from far mountains
At the wave of my hand, moving with the wind, the holy woman
      dances lithely on the pond trailing her scarf
In the starlight, I walk in the depths . . . my reflection broken
      among leaves in the water

May 10, 2011, Rikaze, Tibet

SOARING DOVE

That dove, spotlessly white, red-rimmed eyes . . . enigmatic
When it changes direction mid-flight,
      you hear an ear-delighting coo
Raise your head to watch her in the distance,
      like a lost soul appearing and disappearing
She stretches her wings to reach a vantage point in the cosmos
In the long night, on the far side of the light, she closes her eyes
Her talons grip on a firm rock as if grabbing hold of a lover
Like a horse reaching its destination,
      she flounces and fluffs her feathers
Now, she's like clay of God that can be molded into any shape
A dove transformed into stone at daybreak is an ancient problem
It has nothing to do with whether or not a world dies
The fluffy, pliant chest of the dove is like the flower of a century
Tempting and voluptuous, yet nobody derides it
Like memories from early childhood of mother baring her breast
The dove flies in a dream, she flies in a heart,
      she flies in a sleepless night
Imagining the softness of yielding flesh one sheds homesick tears
The dove breathes gently and gives off a beautiful scent

April 23, 2011; Hanover, Germany

69

RED SPIDER

Red spider crawling on a leaf, traversing its own little world
Catching sunlight, its blood-red glint makes the mind recoil
Tiny mandibles grab anything, like a capturer of the cosmos
Slowly spitting thread, laying its centurial trap
Wind tugs at the sky-spanning web—time for all to look up
All creatures are God's prey, maybe even His enemies
At times the red spider swings, at times it dashes, at times it hesitates
At times looks lovely, at times sinister, at times grieving
Fields at times are barren, landforms dark, rivers dry
Red spider crawls on a leaf, no thought of time lost or wrong turns
Sunbeams through silk illumine distant scenes, shine into a forest
Thousands of life forms flit in and out of sight among branches
From low places heading toward an elevation, from base to noble
Red spider crawls on a leaf, like a master who keeps his skills hidden
Once it crawls behind a leaf, our world starts turning brown
Freshets of rain roil through sky and earth and forest

May 10, 2012

Notes on the Poems

Page 13: Both the Northern and Southern Hemisphere have an 89th parallel. It is the parallel closest to the poles.

Page 33: "on criss-cross paths" - Here the poet uses the phrase "paths shaped like the word 田 (tián)" to mean "crisscross paths."—Tr.

Page 45 - Mani cairns are found in ethnically Tibetan regions of China. Stones are painted or carved with the mantra "om mane padme hum" and piled up in huge numbers to make these cairns. One of the largest, the "Gana Cairn" in Xinzhai, Yushu Prefecture of Qinghai, is estimated to contain over one billion inscribed stones.

Page 49: Big Bell Temple, or Da Zhong Temple, is a Buddist temple located in Beijing, China.

Page 59 - "a plump duck" - In Chinese slang, "duck" could refer to a man who depends upon a woman for his livelihood.—Tr.

Page 66 - Wuyingren, literally "man with no shadow" is also the Chinese term for an "ascian" in MapleStory—a popular internet game. "Ascian" is the Latin word for "one who lacks a shadow." It is also a subclass of characters belonging to the Warrior class in MapleStory. —Tr.

The Chinese *xiangsi-niao* (literally "lovebird") is the silver-eared mesia (*Leiothrix argentum*), which is native to Southeast Asia and the Indian subcontinent. The Chinese lovebird is different from the Western lovebird of the genus *Agapornis*.

Page 68; Mercury flowers are flowers from a genus of flowering plants in the spurge family.

The Tibetan fox is a semi-aquatic canid found near water sources such as the Tibetan Plateau.

The Poet

Luo Ying is the pen name of Huang Nubo, who holds a Ph.D. in Literature from Peking University. He authored the novel *Conch of Mount Everest* and the scholarly monograph, *Nothingness and Blossoming: Reconstructing Modernity in Contemporary Chinese Poetry* (Peking University Press). He has published eleven poetry collections including *7+2 :A Mountain Climber's Journal* (White Pine Press) and *Memories of the Cultural Revolution* (Oklahoma University Press), both published in English translation in the United States. His work has also been translated into French, German, Japanese, Korean, Turkish, Mongolian, Spanish and Icelandic.

He is an intrepid mountaineer and a key member of the Explorers Club in New York City. He has successfully climbed the highest peaks on all seven continents, including three ascents of Mount Everest, and reached the North and South Poles on foot. A successful Chinese real estate developer and entrepreneur, he founded and remains chairman of Beijing Zhongkun Investment Group. He has also founded the Zhongkun Group Poetry Development Fund, the Sino-Japanese Poetry Fund, and the Sino-Icelandic Poetry Fund. He serves as vice-president of the China Poetry Association and standing deputy-dean of the China Poetry Institute at Peking University, where he started the first Poet-in-Residence program.

Luo Ying has initiated many international poetry festivals and has established exchanges among Chinese and South American poets. He also established the Zhongkun International Poetry Prize, sponsored by the China Poetry Institute at Peking University.

Currently engaged in a ten-year plan to visit all the world's cultural heritage sites, Luo Ying strives to protect the environment and its creatures. He is a board member of WildAid International and chairman of WildAid China.

Luo Ying's website is www.luoying.me.

The Translator

Denis Mair has translated the work of numerous Chinese poets into English, including the volumes *Reading the Times: Poems of Yan Zhi* (Homa & Sekey Books, 2012) and *Selected Poems by MaiCheng* (Shearsman Books, 2008). He also translated Luo Ying's *7+2 A Mountain Climber's Journal* (White Pine Press, 2020). His translation of Ying's *Diary of a Sent-Down Youth* is forthcoming from White Pine Press.